Requirements Elicitation for the Development and Implementation of a B2B Mobile App. Writing A Consultant Bid Report

Sixbert SANGWA

Bibliographic information published by the German National Library:

The German National Library lists this publication in the National Bibliography; detailed bibliographic data are available on the Internet at http://dnb.dnb.de.

ISBN: 9783346399106
This book is also available as an ebook.

© GRIN Publishing GmbH
Nymphenburger Straße 86
80636 München

Print and binding: Books on Demand GmbH, Norderstedt, Germany
Printed on acid-free paper from responsible sources.

The present work has been carefully prepared. Nevertheless, authors and publishers do not incur liability for the correctness of information, notes, links and advice as well as any printing errors.

GRIN web shop: https://www.grin.com/document/1008017

Management Project

Consultancy Bid Report

Sixbert SANGWA

December 2018

SUMMARY

As the technology develops, companies are adopting emerging technologies in their business model. Mobile Business-to Business (B2B) application is currently an innovative technology that fosters business-customer interactions. However, the Choice of business-to-business (B2B) commerce requires highly customized applications developed for specific needs, offering highly specialized, service-oriented and solution-based software components, systems, and digital tools, aiming for a fast and accurate decision support system. This forces organization willing to implement mobile application as part of its project, to start with a careful requirement elicitation process which helps to determine necessities and serve as basis for strategic decisions.

One of the companies that has discovered the importance of implementing a B2B mobile app in their operations is the company X, an SME in the food industry that supplies food products to catering companies.

This document is a report bid proposal for conducting a scoping study that determines the necessary requirements for development and implementation of a B2B mobile application for the client, company X. The report focuses on different things that the client should consider before investing resources into the project, helps the company to make the necessary preparations and serves as a strategic decision making tool. The approach presented are techniques and methods approved by industry experts as well as case study-based experiences. The bid introduces the appropriate methods to investigate the suitable functionalities of the B2B application (Functional requirements), conditions necessary for the adequacy of the implementation of the application in the structural conditions of the company X (Structural requirements) and the resources requirements for the project. While the study will be conducted within six (6) months, a Gantt chart is used to indicate which activities should be performed; as well as where and when, in order to complete the study efficiently and effectively. Lastly, the contribution section acknowledges the benefits of the methods/techniques chosen, their relevance to the project and the reasons why they were adopted in the study.

Key Words: Requirements elicitation techniques, B2B application, software engineering, requirements engineering process, mobile app features and functionality.

Table of Contents

1. INTRODUCTION

In recent decades, there has been a rapid growth and development of information and communication technologies, especially the web 2.0 interactive technologies that dramatically influenced how people communicate (Okello, 2015). Since the introduction of mobile smartphone in 2004, there has been revolution of information flow especially in terms of business. Since then, smartphones and mobile applications outnumbered laptops and desktops (Yoni, 2016). While there has been growing possession and use of internet-capable devices such as laptops, smartphones, tablets, etc. on different workplaces (OECD, 2004, Dahlstrom et al., 2015; Daniel, 2016); technology has changed business conditions, customer behavior and market opportunities by allowing connectivity and electronic collaboration between businesses and their customers. For example, the study conducted in 2017 indicated that people spend, on average, 2 hours per day using their phones, compared to 97 minutes they spend with their friends and families (Kapil, 2017). This allowed people to become familiar with different mobile software which became easier to use and cheaper (Green and Hannon, 2007). These increasingly popular innovations are continually forcing companies of all sizes to re-evaluate their priorities and rethink the use of technology to engage their audiences through the so-called Business-to-business applications (B2B) (Kuhr, 2017). Today that users spend more and more time on mobile applications (Alin, 2015), B2B applications are becoming important business tools that drive customer relationship management where the most successful companies are taking advantages of mobile applications to reach different business goals (Kapil, 2017; Chris, 2016).

The potential implication today is "If you are not able to reach your audience through mobile or you are not providing a satisfactory mobile experience, you will miss out on your customers."

The current client, company X, is a SME in food sector that provides food products to catering companies. Being aware of these trends, the client is looking for a consultant to undertake a scoping study to determine the necessary requirements for developing a mobile B2B app. This application is believed to promote company visibility, create a Direct Marketing Channel, Provide Value to the company Customers, Build Brand and Recognition, Improve Customer Engagement, and help the company to stand out from the Competition and Cultivate Customer Loyalty (Dan, 2017; Rose, 2017). However, in order to succeed, experts advise that implementers should carefully identify and clearly define relevant requirements beforehand (Olga, 2018).

Like Veronica et al. (2014), the development and integration of software applications in enterprises requires the prior identification and careful analysis of different functional and non-functional requirements. Since our client wants to conduct a study that examines these requirements, the purpose of this paper is to suggest to our client, based on their project objectives, appropriate methods for studying these requirements using appropriate and approved methods that comprehensively map evidences across a range of industrial studies designed to inform future research practice, programs and policy.

1.1. Study Objectives

As highlighted above this study project regards the identification of the necessary requirements for the development of a mobile B2B application. Keeping in mind that the study methodologies build on one another, as discussed above, three types of necessities will be studied:

Objective 1: Identification of the functional requirements of the mobile B2B application in the food market for catering companies. This will be done through market and stakeholder analysis and software benchmarking as well as the security requirements analysis.

Objective 2: Identification of the structural requirements for the programming and implementation of the application in the current structure and capabilities of the company, by conducting a system environmental analysis, personnel analysis and risk identification and analysis.

Objective 3: Identify the resource requirements that the client needs to raise for the programming, implementation and operation of the mobile B2B application, which will be achieved through project time planning and Life-Cycle Cost Analysis.

1.2. Methodology

While the failure or success of most software depends on the quality of requirements gathered, the quality of requirements also depends on the techniques that were used to gather those requirements (Goel & Kulkarni, 2017). According to Fahad (2016), the availability of internal and partners data is one of the key success points for the growth

4

of the B2B environment. Knowing that in software development there are both requirements elicitation and requirements engineering (Dolly & Khanum, 2016), the study will use industry-based studies and case studies to understand different project necessities. Since the requirements elicitation is regarded as the most important step in shaping software engineering (Hickey & Davis, 2004; Gunda, 2008; Rafiq et al. ,2017; Lent, 2018), the study will focus on the requirement elicitation approach where different mobile B2B App users, customers, and stakeholders will be approached as advised by Dolly & Khanum (2016). While the study will critically analyze and justify methodologies used, an organization wide assessment tour is believed to provide relevant information required for the development and content of the app. It is believed that by attempting to properly identify these requirements, they will improve their quality and, ultimately, the quality of the final software application.

2. SUPPORTING EVIDENCES

This section discusses the context as well as the individual processes corresponding to the approaches chosen for the study of all the requirements necessary for the client's project. Since different established techniques will be used to gather information such as interviews, prototyping and brainstorming as well as recommended less common techniques such as market analysis, team discussion and the use of model users (Rafiq et al., 2017); the consultant must maintain constant communication with the client throughout a requirements elicitation process so that any change in the client's requirements can be integrated as soon as it has been identified to make the study more appropriate.

This is inspired by the experience of Rafiq et al. (2017) who indicated that requirements elicitation is an ongoing process where many changes occur during and after the requirements identification process, hence communication with the business executives is strongly recommended.

2.1. Objective 1: Functional Requirements

As early mentioned, mobile has become a new frontier in the current dynamic and complex business environment where technology continues to shrive. Because mobile devices are used on a move, all businesses, either big or small will eventually need to develop a mobile app to allow customers to reach them from wherever they are (Ali, 2013).

Oinas-Kukkonen et al (2013) distinguish two types of mobile applications: "highly goal-driven and entertainment-focused". According to them, the difference lies in their features and functionalities, which vary depending on the app purposes. What's more challenging on today's marketplace is developing an application that adds value to your business.

Recognizing that mobile B2B applications face market acceptance problems due to lack of user-focus and relevance (Sadler, 2005), to succeed on marketplace, mobile B2B applications are best examined their functioning and the value they provide to their users.

This study, which analyzes the functional requirements of the B2B application, will advise on the functional direction of the application and present important value creating characteristics that correspond to purchasing strategies and business-customer relationships. More specifically the study will examine mobile application platform, usability and security.

2.1.1. Market and Stakeholder Analysis

A. Market Analysis

For the success of the B2B application, it is very crucial to conduct a market analysis based on the app's objectives, in order to make better decisions (Sadler, 2005). An in-depth knowledge of the target market and the characteristics of the customers is essential to decide on the design of the application and the appropriate functionalities adapted to the market. Understanding market needs will help app designers to develop a unique marketing plan and features.

Market research helps to understand the needs, expectations, or preferences of customers, which is essential for determining the integration pathways of an application. If business application designers are unable to understand users in their practices, the mobile application fails to represent this knowledge in the design process and, as a result, the likelihood of acceptance decreases (Robertson, 2005). This is why in order apply user-centric approaches to IT system design, it is strongly advised to carefully research the market and understand its target customers profile.

Market analysis provides an idea of the available operating systems and hardware that can support the application, determine the affordability or willingness and ability of customers to use a mobile application. In this regard, the study will indicate the potential users of the application and their characteristics in order to determine whether the app will run from existing devices or new device, the required user friendly features, the level of transactions that can be made via the application, the aspect of the application to which the public will be authorized to access or be restricted, etc.

Additionally, the market analysis is important to describe project stakeholders and present comparative advantages in order for the company X to launch a successful initiative.

B. Stakeholder analysis

Part of the market assessment focuses particularly on stakeholder analysis, an essential process of requirements elicitation which recognizes that organizations work in complex social landscape where many social actors can influence their work (Eversole, 2018). While on the general sense, stakeholder is any organization / individuals that have a stake or can affect or be affected by a business (Ryan, 2014), in software engineering stakeholders are individuals, groups or organizations that can influence or be influenced by either the development or the use of an application system whether directly or indirectly (Sharp et al. 1999, Chibesakunda, 2015). This practical tool helps to identify potential stakeholders and define their specific needs and expectations for the intended software in order to work effectively with them.

Stakeholder analysis starts with the identification of potential stakeholders, their characteristics and assess their degree of influence so as to develop a strategy to manage and/or engage them. This stakeholder identification provides detailed understanding of the social context and organizational outcomes, hence Eversole (2018) advises to involve clients with extended knowledge about the internal and external proceedings. According to Sharp et al. (1999), this step focuses on the baseline stakeholder which maps both internal and external users, legislators, developers as well as decision makers, the software lifecycle taken into account.

In order to ensure comprehensive involvement of relevant stakeholders and to understand their requirements from the start, it is important to communicate with stakeholders through individual discussions or structured meetings. While not all stakeholders are equally important to the software project, it is advisable to make prioritization and produce a stakeholder matrix that shows their priorities, objectives and contributions.

2.1.2. Software Benchmark Testing

While there are different business applications on market, developed for smartphones and compatible with different operating systems, these applications provide different user-experience that is linked to customer satisfaction (Pizzutillo, 2015). Mobile phones like other pervasive devices also suffer from resource shortages and in this regards Rwassizadeh (2017) advises businesses to carry out a software benchmarking exercise when developing their business applications and before engaging in e-commerce market.

Benchmarking Software Development is the process of collection and comparing data from multiple sources to determine if teams are working as efficiently as possible. In our case, the process examines whether there are existing practices in the market which match our stakeholder objectives.

By comparing the company's operations with equivalent in the industry leaders, the process helps to identify important information for operations improvement, hence it can be seen as a competitive analysis which not only explores best practices but also consult software companies to explore most accurate engaging features. This helps to set the functional requirements of the client on the level that enables him to gain competitive advantages against rivals on both the quality and technology.

As long as the competitors and software companies are concerned, the process starts by needs assessment, Industry/Domain Classification, Collection of qualitative data from acknowledgeable market databases, special software benchmarking reports or from software manufacturers in relevant industry. Once data is collected, the information is normalized and purified. The analysis should compare identified stakeholder objectives with benchmark elaborated in order to set final requirements that the mobile B2B application should fulfil in order to acquire competitive advantages on the market. Finally, the benchmark report should highlight improvement recommendations (Pizzutillo, 2015).

2.1.3. Security Requirements analysis

As mobile applications become a central part of how businesses operate, security is critical to the development of mobile applications (Lent, 2018). The security requirements for enterprise applications are the same as those for mobile applications because people outside the organization routinely take sensitive data. Not only does this mobile tend not to be secure or lost, but people also exchange information on an insecure network, which requires finding requirements to determine how to protect the data.

Pizzutilo (2015) highlighted the difficulty of protecting data on a device that does not belong to an organization, but Lent (2018) emphasizes its importance and requirements. It is therefore essential to consider these constraints by limiting the visibility of personal data while maintaining the visibility of the company's data in order to prevent any loss of data.

The study will therefore present important security requirements for authentication and authorization, offline data allocation, file system protection, hardware and network options and resources.

As advised by software experts (Jeon, Rhee & Won, 2012; Schurr, 2018), the consultant will use the Common Vulnerability Scoring System (CVSS) to capture the main characteristics of vulnerabilities and risks related to mobile applications, define the severity, prioritize the elements to be corrected and propose vulnerability management processes.

2.2. Objective 2: Structural Requirements

This part shows how the study will explore the structural requirements that the Company X will have to fulfill to develop and manage a successful mobile B2B application in today's complex environment.

It focuses on identifying the IT skills required of company personnel and any other ability to control risks or deviations by itself or with the help of external stakeholders.

2.2.1. System Environmental Analysis

Research indicates that the number of mobile B2B applications is growing, with each application competing with millions of leading apps. As companies continue to develop applications to keep their customers engaged via mobile phones, it is difficult to incorporate new application modifications with specialized features into existing IT systems and interfaces in order for the app to be discovered, downloaded and provide the best user experience to retain customers for a long time (eMarketer, 2016).

In this regard and keeping in mind that software benchmarking indicates functional requirements that meet the objectives of the stakeholders and review their priorities in the stakeholder matrix; the environmental scan of the system should explore the ease of development and implementation of these requirements within the IT system environment of the company X. As advised by other industry professionals (Bedell, 2013; Lent, 2018), the elicitation process is the most recommended in view of the current needs to integrate a new B2B application into the existing IT system environment. Integrating changes into this system environment of interactive systems that are part of the operational enterprise (Liu et al., 2016) and which involves other entities (Bedell, 2013), creates constraints that need to be examined to see if the customer can manage them.

Therefore, the consultant will work with different stakeholder groups to determine the specific requirements for the new system. The study should also explore the necessities and compare the systems and interfaces before and after a new application and produce a graph to understand affected modules and the interface tools needed to enable the exchange of data and the operational use of the application. It should also reveal existing IT services and support processes to consider when developing and implementing a mobile B2B application.

In order to do so, the process merely has to be conducted through interviews with application owners or IT leaders so as to get relevant detailed information about systems and with external providers if IT processes are administered by external stakeholders.

2.2.2. Personnel Analysis

Referring to the identified functional requirements that need to be integrated and implemented and how these will interact with the system environment, the personnel analysis will examine whether the Company X has the necessary staff resources to implement it (Andrea et al., 2017). While the consultant needs to consider how this project is integrated within the organization and how the teams are structured; this project for developing and implementing a mobile B2B application is only executable if the client has the required employees with the appropriate skill sets (MindFit Consulting,2018)

One of the key ways to build staff capacity is to provide appropriate training for developers and staff, but this may be a little more difficult for this new engineering project. So, a comparison of tasks and roles within the client organization will help to understand the specific requirements of the staff i.e. personnel need assessment (OECD, 2004).

What marks the first step in this project is carrying role planning where roles must be defined based on the identified functional requirements and the results of the statement environmental analysis. However, project roles should also be embedded within the client's organizational hierarch; technical and administrative tasks taken into account (Jucan, 2013).

Since the project brings new tasks / responsibilities and may impose additional roles, the client's organizational capacities should be considered based on the information gathered internally such as personnel data base, organigram and possible job descriptions. In this case, interview with the CEO, the senior management team or any other concerned senior person would be insightful (Gavin, 2014; Rose 2017).

2.2.3. Risk Identification and Analysis

According to Vivian (2016), the risks are the uncertainty or deviations from the objectives of the project, which, once they have occurred, can affect a project in a positive or negative way. Because the risks are caused by different things, whether by internal or external factors; they can also occur at different stages of the project; hence a need to identify as many risks as possible for the project in order to be prepared for any problem (Haughey, 2015). Although each project has its own risks, it is the responsibility of managers to manage these risks on a daily basis. However, absolute risk elimination is impossible, but "a conscientiously conducted risk management approach is one of the major steps in the preparation of each project" (Passenheim, 2009). While Company X looks for the outcomes and enduring benefits of the application in future, it is essential to identify, map and communicate possible risks that the project may face so that the client can decide on the level of risk that he can take.

The process of identifying risks draws insights from other previous clients' projects, taking into consideration the checklist of possible project risks provided by Boehm (1991). It has to use brainstorming meetings in order to explore different angles. Once risks that may affect either the project or its outcomes have been identified, they have to be analyzed to understand the consequences they may create, and ranked according to their magnitude. A matrix with an ordinal scale (high, medium, low) indicating the probability of risks and their magnitude should be provided, as well as indications of how these anticipated risks can be addressed. This helps determine whether the client is capable of managing the risks.

2.3. Objective 3: Resource Requirements

Having looked at different structural requirements to implement the project in a way that meets stakeholder objectives identified earlier, the consultant should now examine the required resources for the implementation of this B2B mobile application. These resources may be quantifiable equipment, facilities or any other element necessary for the execution of the project (Bpayne &Watt, 2018; Hartney, 2017). More specifically, in software engineering, equipment can designate hardware, software or other tools of different updated versions that the company can buy or rent (Jennifer, 2017). Although the resources are storable or non-storable, they must remain available during the life of the project, unless they are depleted by use, but can also be replenished by the project tasks that produce them. Furthermore, the study will also examine the project life and the financing required by the client to implement it.

2.3.1. Project Time Planning

Like other projects, the B2B application is a client undertaking in software engineering where one of the most renowned temporal requirement is project time planning which provides an estimate of time the company X needs to spend on the project. Since a project is said to be successful when it meets the needs of its entire stakeholders (Haughey, 2015), time planning has been considered the most important step in software engineering because of the complexity of the industry, which presents many uncertainties (Ludovic & Marle, 2008; Bpayne &Watt, 2018).

In the software industry, time planning begins with breaking down the network-based work to estimate the amount of time required and to develop the schedule (Jennifer, 2017). This step requires in-depth knowledge of software programming, which relies on experienced software engineers, but the step can also be informed by previous case studies that are critical to estimating the timing required for all network activities.

Once all network-based activities are identified, the next step is to organize them according to a logical sequence and their dependencies (Project Management Institute, 2013). Estimating the duration of each activity is essential to determine the total duration of the task and becomes useful in drawing a network diagram, which results in a detailed Gantt chart (Al-Naeem et al., 2005 p41-70). Furthermore, by assigning costs and resources to each activity, a detailed plan is now elaborated and the analysis of resource constraints is easily made.

2.3.2. Life Cycle Cost
Analysis

The Project Life Cycle Cost Analysis (LCCA) is one of the recommended processes that determines the economic value of a project by analyzing initial costs and future costs such as maintenance, reconstruction, rehabilitation, restoration and resurfacing a project (Douglass, 2016). This technique helps companies make cost-effective investment decisions over the life of the investment. Although projects in software industry incur costs that are not obvious without in-depth analysis, the LCCA seems an appropriate technique to determine the total financial requirement for the B2B application, because it does not only show initial costs but also the follow-up costs over the project life.

According to Fuller (2016), Life-cycle cost analysis (LCCA) is a method for assessing the total cost of a project from project planning to the total duration of the project. It takes into account the labor, material and other different types of costs, which are normally divided in five categories: direct, indirect, contingent, intangible as well as external costs (Norris, 2001). While time planning process breaks down the work into different stages, the LCCA technique uses the results to calculate the project total costs, which are obtained by summing up costs of individual activities. Individual activity cost is estimated based on the current market prices, either for hourly wage or for relevant tools (Najadat, Alsmadi and Shboul, 2012). While the software life cycle is divided into different phases, the total switching costs are discounted to future values based on the functional steps of the software (Alwan, 2015)

It is very important to note that costs may vary over time, which may result in the risk of relying on LCCA data rather than using it as an orientation tool. Passenheim (2009) advises adjusting costs during implementation based on more detailed and accurate performance experiences, thereby improving reliability.

3. STUDY GANTT CHART

As discussed above, the study will take different methods to execute different tasks that are interdependent. Because each task has a given implementation time and duration and follows a sequential order due to their interdependencies, using a study Gantt chart is an advisable way to illustrate how the project will run (Chinampton, 2011). Gantt chart is a project management tool that illustrates the project tasks against the time. It indicates all project activities, their schedule that highlights the duration of individual activities and their dependencies, the possible overlap of activities as well as the start and end date of the entire project (Dominic, 2018).

The study focuses on the key project activities within the duration of six (6) months equivalent to 24 weeks. The Gantt chart ensures that planned activities are workable and that contingency plan is possible in case the schedule meets some obstacles. The study starts with kick of meetings to initiate the project. These meetings introduce the project to relevant parties; present all involved and responsible people and the details about the project (Aston, 2016; Bpayne &Watt, 2018). However, continuous communication between Consultant and client will remain intact in order to ensure that the study is adequate. Furthermore, the study is divided into different sections corresponding to a set of objectives that are intended to meet the client requirements. Each objective is met using a particular method and/ or appropriate analytical tool. This is very important because it doesn't only indicate tasks to be done but also their practicability by showing the sequential order of activities in order to ensure timely delivery of the entire project.

In the below Gantt chart, activities are represented in two dimensions whereby the vertical axis shows the sequential activities needed to achieve an objective and to effectively and efficiently execute the project. The horizontal axis shows the implementation time and duration for each activity. This is very important to help client and other stakeholders understand the major project steps, agree on expectations that the company X will be expecting from the consultancy during the scheduled meeting for feedback and progress report.

Study Gantt Chart

Timeframe (6 months = 24 Weeks)

Oct-18 | Nov-18 | Dec-18 | Jan-19 | Feb-19 | Mar-19 (Week 1 – Week 24)

Objectives	Activity Description	Duration in weeks
All	**Kick Starting**	
	Kick off meetings for welcome and project brief	2
	Review of the Company portfolio	1
Objective 1	**Identification of Functional Requirements**	11
	Market Analysis	5
	Understand customer characteristics, experience and preferences	2
	Identify existing application systems	1
	Conduct a market survey	2
	Analyze and compile the information of the survey	4
	Stakeholder Analysis	3
	Identify potential project stakeholders	2
	Meeting and Interview with key stakeholders	2
	Identify and document stakeholder priorities	1
	Stakeholder matrix	3
	Software evaluation	3
	Collecting data from reliable sources	2
	Data analysis and documentation	1
	Analysis of the app Security Requirements	1
	Assessing common vulnerability for B2B App system	1
	Recommendation on app security protection requirements	6
Objective 2	**Identification of Structural Requirements**	3
	System Environment Analysis	1
	Interview with key informants (KIIs)	2
	Needs analysis and documentation	2
	Personnel Analysis	1
	Project role planning	1
	Current Structural and role analysis in consultation with the CEO	1
	Final role and structural propositions	3
	Risk Analysis	2
	Identification of possible project risks	1
	Risk evaluation and ranking depending on their magnitude	1
	Risk mitigation or contingency propositions	5
Objective 3	**Identification of Resources Requirements**	3
	Project time planning	2
	Identification of major network-based activities	1
	Activity breakdown and time estimation	1
	Draw a Gantt chart	2
	Life cycle cost analysis	2
	Identifying different types of project costs	1
	Summing up activity costs	
Final Steps	**Producing the study report**	22
	Producing the draft report	3
	Progress reports and Evaluation meetings	1
	Submission of the final study report	1
	Presentation of results	1
	Amendment of feedback and recommendations	

Source: Own figure

4. CONTRIBUTIONS

This section brings together industry evidences and sector research as well as previous case studies to show how the chosen techniques contribute to the identified study objectives and to the satisfaction of the client's overall requirements.

4.1. Objective 1: Functional Requirements

Functional requirements describe the B2B application system functionalities or services (Veronica et al., 2014). Based on the project scope, the study will concentrate on the business, stakeholder and user requirements for which the following requirements determination methods are recommended by previous industrial researches.

4.1.1. Market and Stakeholder Analysis

To add value to project performance and obtain project success, market analysis is an important managerial decision-making tool that help managers to achieve their organization purpose (Rolstadås et al. 2015).

In the food sector, many applications developed do not provide a return on investment, because developers do not consider certain market prospects (Kelly, 2016). As advised by Haugestad (2015), a market analysis conducted before B2B app development is an essential value-centric approach that helps to determine the best features that facilitate interaction between prospects and salespeople and offer opportunities for supply-ordering. In this study, a market research will help convey information about the end users of the application, their level of exposure to modern technology, and the precise level of application technology that they can cope with to meet their expectations.

On the other hand, in business-to-business sales, it is generally recognized that multiple stakeholders are usually involved in the decision-making process (Apollo, 2018). In this regard, a stakeholder analysis is important for company X to identify those stakeholders likely to affect/influence the mobile B2B app project, and then manage their different demands through the communication and development of the objectives of the proposed project (Kevin 2018). This does not only help to understand stakeholder requirements but also allow for continuous improvement.

Therefore, the study will approach identified potential stakeholders to inquire about insights on the app design and features in order to ensure that the project objectives correspond with the stakeholder expectations, which determines the project success (Bpayne &Watt, 2018; Kevin, 2018). At the same time, market and stakeholder analysis will also map available market opportunities, highlight the B2B application success criteria, customer or market needs, and reveal potential business risks.

4.1.2. Software Evaluation

One of the most important steps in B2B application development is benchmarking applications, a process that compares the application's performance with its industry counterpart and allows you to see an application objectively and have a realistic vision of its potential (Pizzutillo, 2015; Jordan, 2018).

While copying other apps is commonly distinguished in software development, literature shows that there are some functionalities that are appropriate to a given industry. Identifying those features that can make your business stand out is as good as innovating the foundation that your competition has built by making it yours and by making it better. (Jordan, 2018). In this regard, benchmarking will help the company X improve its IT processes by discovering some functions or features that may be missing or not being used often. It has been argued that a mobile application benchmark reveals different functional requirements, necessary for practical implementation, which would not otherwise be detected by a simple process of market or stakeholders analysis (Rwassizadeh, 2017); hence, a benchmarking exercise will essentially reveal the most engaging features and best practices in the industry to eventually increase both the install and usage retentions.

4.1.3. Security Requirements analysis

In the field of software engineering, especially business application development, security is essential for determining requirements because the security requirements for mobile applications are not the same as for corporate applications (Bedell, 2013).

Since there has been an increasing leak of confidential business information via mobile devices, it is very important to carefully consider security requirements before developing a mobile app in order to be able to identify, analyze and manage attacks performed by different threats agents (Jeon, Rhee & Won, 2012). These security requirements are essential for mobile applications to implement organization-defined out-of-band authentication, apply organization-defined limitations to the integration of data types into other types, and protect privacy and security as well as the integrity of the information transmitted (Schurr, 2018).

The importance of mobile security requirements was emphasized by the US National Institute of Standards and Technology (NIST, 2015) and who recommend careful requirements elicitation so that the app benefits should outweigh its risks. Once these requirements are well studied, application risks and vulnerabilities are reduced (Christina, 2015).

4.2. Objective 2: Structural Requirements

4.2.1. System Environmental Analysis

Looking from the innovation system perspective, this approach is strongly recommended because of its ability to evaluate the factors that prompt the Company X to adopt new technologies as well as potential obstacles in terms of new system needs. In this context, we will mainly study long-term and large-scale technological developments and, in particular, the approach will help us to conclude on the skills required of staff as well as the possible IT risks, because different IT environments require sets of specific skills to ultimately reduce the risk of failure.

Given that poor human interactions, organizational politics and IT technical problems as well as poor adoption of software engineering practices have been at the root of most software project failures in Nigeria (Egbokhare, 2014), as was also the case for Paderborn Baskets, a German basketball team (Walid, 2017); they can be avoided by in-depth analysis of the client's IT infrastructure. In addition, as was the case for the

24

Greek IT organization specializing in providing services to Greek banks, Krikor (2010) found that the System environmental analysis provides a conclusion on the requirements for services and risk management. Furthermore, the analysis of the system environment benefits users and constitutes the basis for further development and staff analysis.

4.2.2. Personnel Analysis

The potential of a personnel analysis is explained by the laborious nature of the client's project, which includes the development, implementation and maintenance of a mobile B2B application. These three steps, which comprise the entire project, encompass a wide range of services, processes and tools needed to ensure that the built environment will perform the right functions (Don, 2017). They therefore need qualified personnel to carry out their day-to-day activities, including designers, developers, testers, administrators, managers and maintenance personnel who ensure that reported bugs are fixed and requests for new features are evaluated and implemented; system updates and backups are performed on a regular basis (Dave and David, 2018). In this regard, Egbokhare (2014) recommends elicitation of scoping requirements, based on relevant case studies, to illustrate the staffing needs of Company X.

It has been argued that the provision and appropriate distribution of qualified personnel in the development of software leads to the success of the process (Krikor, 2010). Therefore, personnel analysis not only highlights skill needs, but also helps the client to decide to outsource external work or to restructure internal employees, provided that they have the opportunity to receive appropriate management and onsite user training as well as manuals and online assistance if required.

4.2.3. Risk Identification and Analysis

All projects involve risks. If a potential risk of the project is not identified in advance, then the project may not be completed on time, within budget and in the expected quality (Rajman, 2017). Particularly in software projects, new mobile B2B applications present different risks that come in new forms, which primarily relate to the project in its own context (Ajay, 2007). Given that the client wants to enter a new IT field where high risks are expected due to the involvement of several independent stakeholders and the difficulty of anticipating emerging threats to services (Ahmed, 2017), risk identification and analysis is extremely important in determining whether the client will be able to manage these risks alone (Rajman, 2017). IT experts and researchers point out that risk identification and analysis must be done by project managers before starting any IT project (Taylor, 2006; Rajman, 2017; Carlton, 2017).This makes it possible to understand the possible risks, to document their characteristics and to define the relevant actions to be taken to control these risks (Taylor, 2006). This was confirmed by Pâmela and Caroline (2014), who conducted research on different IT organizations and found that most IT projects failed because of a lack of consideration of certain risk factors, which led to a poor risk management. As the risk assessment process, especially the risk identification stage plays an important role, the approach will provide a broad list of the relevant risks of B2B applications and the countermeasures required to evaluate the capabilities that the company X needs to develop in order to manage the project risks.

Furthermore, the risk analysis is expected to ensure optimistic time and cost estimates, reduce unexpected budget cuts (Liz, 2018), ensure that all stakeholder inputs are captured, clearly understood and integrated, ensure the availability of resource requirements, rapid customers reviews and feedback cycle as well as adaptation to relevant project changes (Haughey, 2015).

4.3. Objective 3: Resource Requirements

Bpayne & Watt (2018) point to three general types of non-functional development constraints that are time, resources, and quality. In practice, it is generally useful to know the volume of the requirements of a given software. This number is useful for assessing the magnitude of a change in requirements, for estimating the cost of a development or maintenance task, or simply for using it as a denominator in other measures.

4.3.1. Project Time Planning

Project time planning plays a key role in determining project requirements and setting delivery deadlines. Therefore, effective project planning plays a crucial role in the success of the project, as inaccurate time estimation can lead to time pressure or late delivery, which affects project costs (Tira, 2018; Liz, 2018). Furthermore, Verner, Evanco &Cerpa (2007) who studied schedule estimation and software project success prediction found that inaccurate time planning was accompanied by inadequate requirements, which rose time constraints. Therefore, in order to avoid poor time planning and associated risks and losses, it is very important to proceed as advised by Liz (2018) by consciously analyzing and estimating time in a reasonable manner.

4.3.2. Life-Cycle Cost Analysis

While Passenheim (2009) points out that costs are major project implementation requirements, Life-Cycle Cost Analysis (LCCA) is one of the best techniques used to assess the overall project's costs alternatives in order to select an appropriate design that ensures the lowest overall costs consistent with its quality and function (Fuller, 2016). This comprehensive technique (Andrea et al. , 2017), which goes through analytical study to estimate all project costs from inception until the project life cycle, should be applied at any IT product conception phase because of its potential to serve as a strategic decision making tool for managers. In this respect, the technique indicates whether the client will be able to mobilize the required resources and help to conclude on the realization of the project.

Several research studies in the software industry prove the popularity and low cost of the LCCA technique compared to other cost estimation techniques (Korpi and Ala-Risku, 2008, Jiran et al.2013, Tannu and Kumar, 2014; Fuller, 2016). While Tripathi and Rai (2016) emphasize the role of cost estimation in software engineering, particularly to determine the success or failure of contract negotiation and project execution, Liming (1997) is absolutely right about the relevance and adequacy of the LCCA because of its ability to reveal hidden costs and reduce uncertainty. Furthermore, David & Anatoly (2006) emphasize its strong necessity for companies without IT background due to their possible lack of experience in estimating software costs.

5. CONCLUSION

This study applies a holistic approach to determine the project requirements, which the client needs to inform his capital investment decision. Since the approach used entails different approved and knowledge-based methods, it has also to be adapted to the client's individual case so that the company X receives the requirements that fits their business. The case studies and research in the software industry are essential to demonstrate the appropriateness on our methods in determining the requirements of a mobile B2B application for our client, which is an SME in food sector. Although the study Gantt chart indicates the constant involvement of the client, the consultant is fully committed to maintaining a close communication with the client, should there be any change in the client's requirements or need for further enhancement.

Because the results of the study will indicate all the functional, structural, financial and non-financial resources needed to create a B2B mobile application; it is believed that the client will be able to decide to buy, build the mobile app himself, or not implement it at all. However, the client's decision should be based on their ability to mobilize the required resources and manage the relevant project risks that may occur over time, with the study providing guiding recommendations.

6. REFERENCES

[1] Ahmed S.Y. (2017). A Review of Risk Identification Approaches in the Telecommunication Domain. [Online]. Available from: https://www.researchgate.net/publication/314392917_A_Review_of_Risk_Iden tification_Approaches_in_the_Telecommunication_Domain [Accessed on 05 October 2018]

[2] Alin Z. (2015). Factors Influencing the Quality of Mobile Applications. Informatica Economica Journal, Vol.18 (1), pp. 131-138. [Online]. Available from: https://doi.org/10.12948/issn14531305/18.1.2014.12 [Accessed on 17 September 2018]

[3] Al-Naeem, Fethi A. Rabhi, Boualem Benatallah and Pradeep K. Ray (2005). Systematic Approaches for Designing B2B Applications. International Journal of Electronic Commerce, Vol. 9, No. 2 (Winter, 2004/2005), pp. 41-70.

[4] Alwan M. (2015). What is System Development Life Cycle? [Online]. Available from: https://airbrake.io/blog/sdlc/what-is-system-development-life-cycle [Accessed on 22 September, 2018]

[5] Andrea Zangiacomi, Jonathan Oesterle, Rosanna Fornasiero, Marco Sacco & Americo Azevedo (2017) The implementation of digital technologies for operations management: a case study for manufacturing apps, Production Planning & Control, 28:16,1318-1331, DOI: 10.1080/09537287.2017.1375142 [Accessed on 06 October 2018]

[6] Apollo B. (2018). In Complex B2B Sales, Stakeholders Have More Than One Dimension. [Online] Available from: https://www.business2community.com/b2b-marketing/in-complex-b2b-sales-stakeholders-have-more-than-one-dimension-02111011 [Accessed on 01 Oct 2018]

[7] Aston B. (2016). Kickoff Meeting: The Complete Guide to Starting Projects Right. [Online]. Available from: https://thedigitalprojectmanager.com/project-kickoff-meeting/ [Accessed on 06 October 2018]

[8] Bedell C. (2013). Mobile apps development: Defining requirements is a whole new ballgame. [Online]. Available from: https://searchsoftwarequality.techtarget.com/feature/Mobile-apps-development-Defining-requirements-is-a-whole-new-ballgame [Accessed on 21 September 2018]

[9] Boehm, B.W. (1991), "Software Risk Management: Principles and Practices", IEEE Software, Vol.8(1), pp. 426-435.

[10] Carlton D. (2017). Competence versus Confidence in IT Project Leadership and its Impact on Project Outcomes [Online]. Available from: http://journalmodernpm.com/index.php/jmpm/article/view/240/0 [Accessed on 05 October 2018]

[11] Chibesakunda M. (2015). Reflective essay for strategic management of projects. Reflections on the BIS Project. Available from: https://www.academia.edu/21041900/REFLECTIVE_ESSAY_FOR_STRATEG IC_MANAGEMENT_OF_PROJECTS_Reflections_on_the_BIS_Project_Stude nt_in_Work_Role [Accessed on 13 October 2018]

[12] Chinampton (2011). Application Development Plans and Gantt chart. [Online]. Available from: http://blog.soton.ac.uk/chinampton/2011/02/14/application-development-plan-and-gantt-chart/ [Accessed on 29 September 2018]

[13]   Chris L. (2016). B2B Mobile Apps: Why your B2B Business Needs To Care About Mobile. [Online].   Available   from: https://www.handshake.com/blog/b2b-mobile-apps   [Accessed   on   17 September 2018]

[14]   Christina C. (2015). NIST releases guide to mobile app security. [Online]. Available   from: https://sdtimes.com/applications/nist-releases-guide-mobile-app-security/ [Accessed on 01 Oct 2018]

[15]   Dahlstrom, E., Brooks, D.C., Grajek, S. and Reeves, J. (2015), ECAR Study of Students and Information Technology, 2015, ECAR, Louisville, CO, p. 47.Available online at: Google Scholar [Accessed on September 17, 2018]

[16]   Dan S. (2017). 7 Reasons Why Small Businesses Need Mobile Apps. [Online].   Available   from: http://app.foundation/7-reasons-why-small-businesses-need-mobile-apps/ [Accessed on 19 September 2018]

[17]   Daniel A. (2016). 5 Effective Uses of Mobile Technology In The Classroom. Available online from: https://elearningindustry.com/5-uses-mobile-technology-in-the-classroom [Accessed on September 15, 2018]

[18]   Dave B. and David T.B. (2018). Chapter 10: Information Systems Development.   [Online].   Available   from: https://bus206.pressbooks.com/chapter/chapter-10-information-systems-development/ [Accessed on 04 October 2018]

[19]   David Elmakis & Anatoly Lisnianski .(2006). Life cycle cost analysis: Actual problem in industrial management, Journal of Business Economics and Management, 7:1, 5-8, DOI: 10.1080/16111699.2006.9636115 [Accessed on 06 October 2018]

[20]   Dolly B. & Khanum M.A. (2016). Requirement Elicitation in Mobile Apps: A   Review.   Available   from: http://ijcsit.com/docs/aceit-conference-2016/aceit201652.pdf [Accessed on 07 October 2018]

[21]   Dominic T. (2018). Gantt chart: Plan your projects like a pro with time saving apps. [Online]. Available from: https://setapp.com/how-to/gantt-chart-for-project-management [Accessed on 06 October 2018]

[22]   Don S. (2017). Facilities operations & maintenance - an overview. [Online].   Available   from: https://www.wbdg.org/facilities-operations-maintenance [Accessed on 04 October 2018]

[23]   Douglass B. Lee (2016). Fundamentals of Life-Cycle Cost Analysis Article in Transportation Research. Record Journal of the Transportation Research   Board.   Available   from: https://www.researchgate.net/publication/240011149   [Accessed   on   22 September 2018]

[24]   Egbokhare F.A. (2014). Causes of Software/Information Technology Project Failures In Nigerian Software Development Organizations. Afr J. of Comp & ICTs. Vol 7, No. 2. Pp 107-110.

[25]   Eric Korpi, Timo Ala-Risku, (2008) "Life cycle costing: a review of published case studies", Managerial Auditing Journal, Vol. 23 Issue: 3, pp.240-261, https://doi.org/10.1108/02686900810857703 [Accessed on 06 October 2018]

[26]   Eversole R. (2018). Stakeholder Analysis. [Online]. Available from: https://www.researchgate.net/publication/327453706_Stakeholder_Analysis [Accessed on 20 September 2018]

[27]   Fahad I. (2016). Systematic mapping study on integration of B2B customers in ERP. Master thesis:Lappeenranta University of Technology. School of Business and Management. DOI: 10.13140/RG.2.2.23561.24166.

[28]   Fuller S. (2016). Life-Cycle Cost Analysis (LCCA). [Online]. Available from: https://www.wbdg.org/resources/life-cycle-cost-analysis-lcca [Accessed on 06 October 2018]

[29]   Gavin F. (2014). Creating mobile apps for b2b sales & marketing.[Online]. Available from: https://www.chiefmarketer.com/creating-mobile-apps-b2b-sales-marketing/ [Accessed on 06 October 2018]

[30]   Green, H. and Hannon, C. (2007), Their Space: Education for a Digital Generation, London. Available at: http://scholar.google.com/scholar_lookup?hl=en&publication_year=2007&issue=3&author=H.+Green&author=C.+Hannon&title=Their+Space%3A+Education+for+a+Digital+Generation& [Accessed on 17 September 2018]

[31]   Gunda S. G. (2008). Requirements Engeneering: Elicitation techniques. [Online]. Available from: http://www.diva-portal.org/smash/get/diva2:215169/fulltext01 ;

[32]   Hartney J. (2017). Types of Project Resources. [Online].Available from: http://www.projectengineer.net/types-of-project-resources/ [Accessed on 22 September 2018]

[33]   Haugestad R. (2015). Innovation Strategy for B2B Mobile Apps: a Value-centric Approach. Master Thesis: Norwegian University of Life Sciences. Available from: https://brage.bibsys.no/xmlui/bitstream/handle/11250/295632/haugestad_master2015.pdf?sequence=4 [Accessed on 01 Oct 2018]

[34]   Haughey D. (2015). Project planning a step-by-step guide. [Online]. Available from: https://www.projectsmart.co.uk/project-planning-step-by-step.php [Accessed on 05 November 2018]

[35]   Hickey, A., & Davis, A. (2004). A Unified Model of Requirements Elicitation. Journal of Management Information Systems, 20(4), 65-84. Retrieved from http://www.jstor.org/stable/40398654 [accessed on 19 September 2018]

[36]   Jennifer B. (2017). Resource Planning for Projects: A Guide. [Online]. Available from: https://www.projectmanager.com/training/resource-planning-for-projects-a-guide [Accessed on 22 September 2018]

[37]   Jeon W., Rhee K. and Won D. (2012).Security Requirements of a Mobile Device Management System. [Online]. Available from: https://www.researchgate.net/publication/267227402_Security_Requirements_of_a_Mobile_Device_Management_System [Accessed on 01Oct 2018]

[38]   Jiran N.s., Mahmood S., Saman M.Z.M. and Noordin M.Y. (2013). Review on Methodology for Life Cycle Costing of Membrane System for Wastewater Filtration. [Online]. Available from: https://www.researchgate.net/publication/272606953_Review_on_Methodology_for_Life_Cycle_Costing_of_Membrane_System_for_Wastewater_Filtration [Accessed on 06 October 2018]

[39]   Jordan M. (2018). Why app benchmarking is essential for your mobile app's success. [Online]. Available from: https://www2.stardust-testing.com/en/why-app-benchmarking-is-essential-for-your-mobile-apps-success [Accessed on 01 Oct 2018]

[40]   Jucan, G. (2013), "People in Senior Project Roles", in: Lock, D. and Scott, L. (eds.), *The Gower Handbook of People in Project Management*. Farnham: Gower.

[41]   Kapil M. (2017). The undeniable importance of mobile applications and its global impact. International Journal of Advanced Science and Research ISSN: 2455-4227, Impact Factor: RJIF 5.12 .Volume 2; Issue 3; May 2017; Page No. 32-36. Available online from: www.allsciencejournal.com [Accessed on 17 September 2018]

[42]   Kevin H. (2018). Principles of Management. [Online]. Available from: http://open.lib.umn.edu/principlesmanagement/chapter/4-6-stakeholders/ [Accessed on 01 Oct 2018]

[43]   Krikor, M. (2010), "IT Project Environment Factors Affecting Requirements Analysis in Service Provisioning for the Greek Banking Sector", Journal of Software Engineering & Applications, Vol.3, pp. 858-868. Available from: 10.4236/jsea.2010.39100 [Accessed on 04 October 2018]

[44]   Kuhr T. (2017). How emerging technologies will affect your business in 2018. [Online]. Available from: https://martechtoday.com/emerging-technologies-will-affect-business-2018-206042 [Accessed on September 17, 2018]

[45]   Lent J. (2018). Software requirements development: FAQ. [Online]. Available from: https://searchsoftwarequality.techtarget.com/feature/Software-requirements-development-FAQ [Accessed on 20 September 2018]

[46]   Liming W. (1997). The Comparison of the Software Cost Estimating Methods. [Online]. Available from: https://www.computing.dcu.ie/~renaat/ca421/LWu1.html [Accessed on 06 October 2018]

[47]   Liu B. et al. (2016).Structural Analysis of User Choices for Mobile App Recommendation. [Online]. Available from: https://arxiv.org/abs/1605.07980 [Accessed on 21 September 2018]

[48]   Liz C. (2018). Project management: time estimates and planning. [Online]. Available from: https://www.projectsmart.co.uk/project-management-time-estimates-and-planning.php [Accessed on 05 October 2018]

[49]   Ludovic-Alexandre Vidal, Franck Marle. (2008).Understanding project complexity: implications on project management. Kybernetes, Emerald. [Online]. Available from: https://hal.archives-ouvertes.fr/hal-01215364/document [Accessed on 22 September 2018]

[50]   MindFit Consulting (2018). Personnel analysis. [Online]. Available from: https://www.mindfitconsulting.com/en/personnelanalysis/ [Accessed on 06 October 2018]

[51]   Najadat H., Alsmadi I. And Shboul Y. (2012). Predicting Software Projects Cost Estimation Based on Mining Historical Data. ISRN Software Engineering. Volume 2012, Article ID 823437, 8 pages http://dx.doi.org/10.5402/2012/823437 [Accessed on 22 September 2018]

[52]   Norris, G.A. (2001), "Integrating life cycle cost analysis and LCA", *The International Journal of Life Cycle Assessment*, Vol.6(2), pp. 118-120.Available from: https://www.researchgate.net/publication/225548796_Integrating_life_cycle_c ost_analysis_and_LCA [Accessed on 22 September 2018]

[53]   OECD (2004), "ICT, E-Business and Small and Medium Enterprises", *OECD Digital Economy Papers*, No. 86, OECD Publishing,

Paris, https://doi.org/10.1787/232556551425 [Accessed on 21 September 2018]

[54]   OECD (2004), "ICT, E-Business and Small and Medium Enterprises", OECD Digital Economy Papers, No. 86, OECD Publishing, Paris. http://dx.doi.org/10.1787/232556551425 [Accessed on September 17, 2018]

[55]   Oinas-Kukkonen, H. & Kurkela, V. 2003, 'Developing Successful Mobile Applications', International Conference on Computer Science and Technology, Cancun, Mexico, pp. 50-4. Available from: https://www.researchgate.net/publication/228785470_Developing_Successful _Mobile_Applications [Accessed on 19 September 2018]

[56]   Okello-Obura, Constant and Ssekitto, Francis, "WEB 2.0 TECHNOLOGIES APPLICATION IN TEACHING AND LEARNING BY MAKERERE UNIVERSITY ACADEMIC STAFF" (2015). Library Philosophy and Practice (e-journal). 1248. http://digitalcommons.unl.edu/libphilprac/1248 [Accessed on September 17, 2018]

[57]   Olga S. (2018). Requirements. Why is it important? [Online]. Available from: https://steelkiwi.com/blog/requirements-why-it-important/ [Accessed on 19 September 2018]

[58]   Pâmela R., Caroline M. (2014). Perceptions of success and failure factors in information technology projects: a study from Brazilian companies. Available from: https://core.ac.uk/download/pdf/82430608.pdf [Accessed on 05 October 2018]

[59]   Passenheim O. (2009), Project Management. Copenhagen: Bookboon. [Online].   Available   from: http://freecomputerbooks.com/Project_Management_by_Passenheim.html [Accessed on 06 October 2018]

[60]   Pizzutillo P. (2015). Software Benchmarks and Benchmarking. [Online]. Available from: https://www.castsoftware.com/blog/software-benchmarks-and-benchmarking [Accessed on 20 September 2018]

[61]   Pouloudi, A. and Whitley, E.A. (1997), "Stakeholder identification in inter-organizational systems: gaining insights for drug use", European Journal of Information Systems, Vol.6 (1), pp. 1-14.

[62]   Project Management Institute (2013), "A Guide to the Project Management Body of Knowledge (PMBOK Guide)", Newtown Square, Pa.: Project Management Institute.

[63]   Rajman M. R. (2017). Project Risk Identification for New Project Manager.[online]. Available from: https://www.projecttimes.com/articles/project-risk-identification-for-new-project-manager.html [Accessed on 05 October 2018]

[64]   Rawassizadeh Reza (2017).Mobile Application Benchmarking Based on the Resource Usage Monitoring. [Online]. Available from: https://pdfs.semanticscholar.org/4204/29735a983126ac0e4165edbba75f11ed e578.pdf [Accessed on 20 September 2018]

[65]   Robertson T. (2005). A useful design tool for mBusiness.[online]. Available   from: https://www.researchgate.net/publication/4167674_Use_scenarios_A_useful_ design_tool_for_mBusiness [Accessed on 19 September, 2018]

[66]   Rolstadås, A., Pinto, J. K., Falster, P., & Venkataraman, R. (2015). Project decision chain. Project Management Journal, 46(4), 6–19.

[67]   Rose E. (2017). The Anatomy of an Effective B2B Mobile App. [online]. Available from: https://www.digitaldoughnut.com/articles/2017/march/the-anatomy-of-an-effective-b2b-mobile-app [Accessed on 06 October 2018]

[68]   Ryan MJ (2014). The role of stakeholders in requirements elicitation. INCOSE Int Symp 24(1):16–26. https://doi.org/10.1002/j.2334-5837.2014.tb03131.x [Accessed on 19 September 2018]

[69]   Sadler K., Robertson T. & Kan M. (2005). Use Scenarios: A Useful Design Tool For mBusiness. [Online]. Available from: https://www.researchgate.net/publication/4167674_Use_scenarios_A_useful_design_tool_for_mBusiness [Accessed on 19 September 2018]

[70]   Sharp H., Finkelstein A. & Galal G. (1999). Stakeholder Identification in the Requirements Engineering Process. Available from: http://discovery.ucl.ac.uk/744/1/1.7_stake.pdf [Accessed on 19 September, 2018]

[71]   Tannu and KumarY. (2014). Comparative Analysis of Different Software Cost Estimation Methods. International Journal of Computer Science and Mobile Computing. IJCSMC, Vol. 3, Issue. 6, June 2014, pg.547 – 557

[72]   Taylor, H. (2006). Risk management and problem resolution strategies for IT projects: prescription and practice. *Project Management Journal, 37*(5), 49–63.

[73]   Tira D. (2018). What Is the Importance of Project Scheduling & Its Role in Business Projects? [Online]. Available from: https://yourbusiness.azcentral.com/importance-project-scheduling-its-role-business-projects-9503.html [Accessed on 05 October 2018]

[74]   Tripathi R & Rai P. K. (2016). Comparative Study of Software Cost Estimation Techniques. International Journal of Advanced Research in Computer Science and Software Engineering. Volume 6, Issue 1, January 2016 ISSN: 2277 128X.

[75]   U. Rafiq, S. S. Bajwa, X. Wang and I. Lunesu, "Requirements Elicitation Techniques Applied in Software Startups," *2017 43rd Euromicro Conference on Software Engineering and Advanced Applications (SEAA)*, Vienna, 2017, pp. 141-144.doi: 10.1109/SEAA.2017.73. Available from: http://ieeexplore.ieee.org/stamp/stamp.jsp?tp=&arnumber=8051340&isnumber=8051309 [Accessed on 09 October 2018]

[76]   Veronica et al. (2014). Requirement analysis method of ecommerce websites development for small-medium enterprises, Case Study: Indonesia. International Journal of Software Engineering & Applications (IJSEA), Vol.5, No.2, March 2014. DOI : 10.5121/ijsea.2014.5202 11.

[77]   Vivian K. (2016). What are the 5 risk management steps in a sound risk management process? [Online]. Available from: http://continuingprofessionaldevelopment.org/risk-management-steps-in-risk-management-process/ [Access on 21 September 2018]

[78]   Walid H. (2017). 5 of the Biggest Information Technology Failures and Scares. [Online]. Available from: https://www.exoplatform.com/blog/2017/08/01/5-of-the-biggest-information-technology-failures-and-scares [Accessed on 04 October 2018]

[79]   Yoni H. (2016). Mobile internet usage surpasses desktop usage for the first time in history. [online]. Available from: https://bgr.com/2016/11/02/internet-usage-desktop-vs-mobile/ [Accessed on 24 November 2018]